REIGNITE YOUR FLAME

COMPANION WORKBOOK TO *REMEMBER YOUR TORCH*

KATIE BISHOP

DRAGON SONG
PRESS

Dragon Song Press
An Imprint of Earth Bishop, LLC., registered in the United States of America.

ISBN: 979-8-9998728-1-4

Author Name: Bishop, Katie.

Titles: Reignite Your Flame: companion workbook to Remember Your Torch: encounters with the supernatural and hidden truths that shape our reality.

Description: Earth Bishop, LLC. Includes self-healing methods and resources.

Subjects: Spirituality. Self-help.

Cover design and interior images by Katie Bishop via Canva.

CONTENTS

PREFACE

Reignite Your Flame is designed to provide more details and instructions on the healing processes I discuss in *Remember Your Torch*.

The goal of this workbook is to provide detailed innerstandings of how you can self-heal and activate your soul remembrance. The exercises are based off of my personal walk-in experiences and my training in natural healing, shamanism, esoteric wisdom, mystery school teachings, and alchemy. By engaging with the practices and exercises outlined, you will be able to:

- Break looping thought patterns
- Break destructive behavioral patterns and addictions
- Heal from trauma
- Embody your higher self
- Feel liberated
- Grant genuine forgiveness
- Bring clarity and focus to your life
- Reactivate the voice of your spirit
- Remember your soul purpose

Tips for maximizing your healing journey

Patience. Be patient with yourself. Healing takes time and cannot be rushed or forced. I recommend working on one area of healing at a time. Be compassionate to yourself, allowing as much time as you need for the healing process.

Honesty. Be painfully honest with yourself. Honor your true feelings and raw emotions without judgement.

Self-care. Be kind and gentle with yourself during the healing process. Take good care of yourself physically, emotionally, and spiritually. Nourish yourself with healthy foods and nurture the needs of your inner child as they arise.

Responsibility. Being a victim of trauma is not your fault, but it is your responsibility to heal from it, which includes respecting and caring for yourself. If you don't respect or care for yourself, then why should anyone else?

Expansion. Approach your healing journey with an open mind and an open heart. Expand your perception of potentials.

Boundaries. You may need to take pauses in certain relationships as you go through the healing steps. Respect the boundaries you may need from others and from society in general as you heal.

Safety. Creating a safe space is foundational for you to purge and process your emotions. Be very selective with whom you share your healing journey and set strong relationship boundaries. Finding a therapist that creates a safe environment for you to share your emotions can help immensely.

Laughter. Make it a point every day to do something that puts a smile on your face or makes you laugh. Laughter is the ultimate medicine.

Personal insights

At the end of each section, I provide insights regarding my personal healing experiences. My intention is to deepen your understanding of the processes by providing context and examples of my experiences.

Notes

The end of each section has space for you to take your own notes as you go through the healing process. I have created the *Remember Who You Are Journal*, available alongside *Remember Your Torch*, to provide you with more space to engage with the exercises in this workbook.

Disclaimer

This workbook is not professional medical advice. I highly recommend seeking regular talk therapy and spiritual guidance to heal trauma in addition to using this workbook. Each person and situation are unique, so there are no one-size-fits-all healing methods. It's important to be open-minded to various modalities and techniques as you go through your healing journey. There are many roads that lead to healing, and this workbook shares the methods that worked best for me and my clients. The healing process is ongoing and happens in layers, so approach your healing as a journey and not a destination. You are a beautiful emanation of the Aviaya in a state of constant creation of self.

FORGIVENESS

What are the foundations of forgiveness?

The power of forgiveness is foundational and woven into many aspects of the self-healing journey. Forgiveness is most often misunderstood as granting tolerance for another's destructive behavior. However, the truth is, forgiveness does not require tolerance for another's destructive behavior. Forgiveness unhooks you from the power the person and the situation hold over you. Forgiveness releases the control the perpetrator once had and restores control to you. In seeing that the perpetrator is broken themselves, it separates you from that person by reclaiming your innocence and sovereignty. Only hurt people hurt people.

Withholding forgiveness is like carrying a giant weight or boulder around behind you. It prevents you from reaching higher levels of spiritual awareness and maturity. It prevents you from reaching fourth density consciousness. Freeing yourself from the weight of unforgivingness is a precious gift you give to yourself and to the collective consciousness.

Granting genuine forgiveness is challenging. Initially, you won't be able to feel true forgiveness, but it will come with time and conscious intention. You will free yourself from the shackles of mind control the person or situation had over you. In other words, you will stop letting that person or situation live rent-free in your mind space.

Process for achieving forgiveness

Through this forgiveness process, you do not need to contact the person to whom you are granting forgiveness. This is a private process, and it is your personal choice whether to share your forgiveness with the person.

Gain perspective. View the situation from a neutral observer standpoint. Try to view the situation from a 360-degree perspective. Identify the areas where you can take responsibility for the situation, if there are any.

Choose. Make the choice to forgive. Set conscious intentions daily to open your heart to forgiveness. Set the intention to free yourself from the control the situation has over you.

Ask. Ask your higher self and Aviaya, Source, God, Creator—whatever higher power you commune with—for assistance and guidance to grant genuine forgiveness. Journal thoughts, downloads, and messages that come to you.

Write. Write a letter to the person you are granting forgiveness to. Write straight from your emotion without a filter, since you will not be sharing this letter. Write down everything you wish you could tell this person. Unleash everything you have been holding inside. Let your thoughts and emotions flow. At the end, tell them you forgive them.

Conduct your ceremony. When you finally feel ready to let go of the weight of unforgiveness, dedicate a time to create a sacred space in silence. Conduct this ceremony outdoors at a fire pit or prepare a small metal bowl, glass of water, and lighter. In this space, light a fire. Then, burn the paper and watch the pain of the situation dissolve, transmute, and purify through the flame. (If not using a fire pit, then burn the paper in the metal bowl and pour water over it to put out the flames.)

Receive. Give thanks for the support of your higher power and open yourself up to receive your traumatized soul parts. Reclaim your innocence and your energy that was once captured by holding onto unforgiveness.

Personal insights

Sometimes the most difficult kind of forgiveness to grant is self-forgiveness. As you progress in your healing journey, you will uncover moments in your life that bring you regret. As I reflected on my life, I was saddened by many moments when I wasn't acting from the heart of my true self, which caused me to create pain for others. Knowing that I inflicted pain on others felt unforgiveable, and I tortured myself with guilt and shame for years.

I finally hit a point in my spiritual journey when I realized I was limiting myself by withholding compassion, forgiveness, and grace for myself. I became motivated to let go and free myself from my mental prison. I found self-forgiveness to be the most challenging kind of forgiveness.

Additionally, the Frequency Override ritual I perform is a beautiful ceremony to consecrate the forgiveness process and shift your consciousness into a higher reality.

Notes

_____

_____

_____

HEALING THE MOTHER WOUND

What is the mother wound?

The mother wound is trauma caused by not getting your childhood needs met physically, emotionally, spiritually, and/or mentally by your mother or maternal caretaker. Neglect, rejection, and abandonment are at the core of the mother wound. The mother wound stems from the lack of nurturing, mirroring, and caring from the mother figure. The mother wound affects both sons and daughters, and it isn't limited to biological mothers; the mother wound can derive from any maternal caretaker, or the lack thereof. Healing from the mother wound is not about shaming the maternal caretaker, since, most often, the wounding is unintentional.

Characteristics of the mother wound include:

- Low self-esteem
- Anxiety
- Depression
- Feeling unworthy
- Insecurity (physical and emotional)
- Nervous system dysregulation

- Obsessive perfectionism
- Relationship problems and codependency
- Self-sabotage
- Unhealthy relationship with food
- Self-deprecating inner voice
- Feeling invisible
- Hyper-independence
- Feeling guilty for having needs

How to heal the mother wound

Healing the mother wound has nothing to do with blaming or judging your mother. You can heal the mother wound without having contact with your mother. In fact, I recommend you perform this process privately, without sharing it with your mother or maternal caretaker.

Step One: Identify

Identify how the mother wound has manifested through you. I recommend focusing on the top three areas where the mother wound affects you. For example: Negative self-talk, the anxious need to constantly please others, and feelings of being unworthy of love and recognition.

Step Two: Purge & release

Carve out a few minutes every day, for at least a week, to purge your raw feelings about your three focus areas. Try to connect to the inner child within you and give them a voice for their true feelings. Write those feelings down. If you don't feel safe keeping the writing, then rip it up afterwards and throw it away.

This step can take time, so be patient and allow yourself enough time to process all the emotions associated with these mother wound manifestations.

You will likely experience anger during this process. It's important to stay physically active to help your body work through the emotions. Somatic yoga can help with releasing the frenetic energy from trauma. I recommend Brett Larkin's YouTube channel for somatic movements.

_____

_____

_____

Step Three: Receive

Set time each day, for at least a week, to visualize your inner child getting their needs met by your mother or maternal caretaker. If this is too difficult, then visualize a spiritual feminine figure providing for you, such as Mother Mary, Mary Magdalene, Green Tara, Quan Yin, Mother Sophia, etc.

You will know the process is working when you have tears streaming down your face from receiving the love your inner child needs.

Step Four: Forgive

Forgiveness is about releasing yourself from the power a hurt or trauma caused you. Being the observer of your mother's past helps you with forgiveness. Take yourself outside your body and observe your mother's history and upbringing. Often, you will discover that her hurts and traumas were never healed. She may never have been loved or cared for properly. Or, perhaps, the pain she inflicted upon you was completely unconscious, and she was under the delusion of our collective mind-controlled false matrix reality.

Step Five: Heal

I like using the power of *Ho'oponopono* based on the work of Dr. Ihaleakala Hew Len. However, I've adjusted the traditional words. Ho'oponopono is a Hawaiian practice of reconciliation and forgiveness; the term means "to make things right."

Find a photo of your mom where you can see her eyes. Light a candle. Look into her eyes in the photo and say three times, "I forgive you. Please forgive me. Thank you. I love you." (Adjust as you feel necessary based on your situation.)

The goal is to do this practice for a minimum of 21 days in a row.

Step Six: Break the chain

Be the mother or parental figure you needed to your children. Be the motherly figure to children that need to feel nurtured and cared for. See your children. Validate them. Honor their individuality. Write about how you are breaking the chain.

_____

_____

_____

Personal insights

Healing the brunt of the mother wound took me years, and I'm still a work in progress. I found great comfort in connecting to the spirits of Mother Mary and Mary Magdalene during this process. I found that I needed a mother figure to look up to and to provide comfort to me. I needed a motherly figure to share my fears and sorrows.

I also tried for years to entertain the idea that I may be able to have a genuine relationship with my mother. But once I grieved the impossibility of that outcome, I stopped hoping and started accepting my mother for who she was. I found great freedom in this process, as it released a tremendous amount of anxiety and unrealistic expectations that I couldn't control.

Notes

_____

_____

_____

HEALING THE FATHER WOUND

What is the father wound?

Similar to the mother wound, the father wound contains the same aspects of not getting your childhood needs met physically, emotionally, spiritually, and/or mentally from your father or paternal caretaker. At its core, the father wound stems from the absence of physical safety and support from a father figure. Other elements include a father figure who displays abuse, constant criticism, and dismissiveness. The father wound affects both sons and daughters, and it isn't limited to biological fathers; the father wound can derive from any paternal figure, or the lack thereof.

Characteristics of the father wound include:

- Suppression of emotions
- Disassociation
- Dismissal of feelings
- Avoidance of intimacy
- Difficulty establishing relationship boundaries
- Anxiety
- Depression

- Shame
- Never feeling good enough
- Anger and aggressive outbursts
- Insecurity (physical and emotional)
- Nervous system dysregulation
- Obsessive need to control
- Relationship attachment disorders

How to heal the father wound

Healing the father wound does not involve judging or shaming paternal figures. The process is similar to healing the mother wound, and you can complete the process in private, without having contact with your father or paternal caretaker.

Step One: Identify

Identify how you have embodied the characteristics of the father wound. I recommend focusing on the top three areas where the father wound affects you. For example: Attachment disorders in relationships, poor anger management, and suppression of emotions.

_____

_____

_____

Step Two: Purge & release

Carve out a few minutes every day, for at least a week, to purge your raw feelings about your three focus areas. Try to connect to the inner child within you and give them a voice for their true feelings. Write those feelings down. If you don't feel safe keeping the writing, then rip it up afterwards and throw it away.

This step can take time, so be patient and allow yourself enough time to process all the emotions associated with these father wound manifestations.

You will likely experience anger during this process. It's important to stay physically active to help your body work through the emotions. Somatic yoga can help with releasing the frenetic energy from trauma. I recommend Brett Larkin's YouTube channel for somatic movements.

Step Three: Receive

Set time each day for at least a week visualizing your inner child getting his/her needs met from your father or paternal caretaker. If this is too difficult, then visualize a spiritual masculine figure providing for you, such as Yeshua, Joseph, Budda, Saint Francis, etc.

You will know the process is working when you have tears streaming down your face from receiving the love your inner child needs.

Step Four: Forgive

Forgiveness is about releasing yourself from the power a hurt or trauma caused you. Being the observer of your father's past helps you with forgiveness. Take yourself outside your body and observe your father's history and upbringing. Often, you will discover that his hurts and traumas were never healed. He may have never been loved or cared for properly. Or, perhaps, the pain inflicted upon you was done completely unconsciously, and he was in survival mode without knowing how to cope with his own pain.

Step Five: Heal

I like using the power of Ho'oponopono based on the work of Dr. Ihaleakala Hew Len. However, I've adjusted the traditional words. Ho'oponopono is a Hawaiian practice of reconciliation and forgiveness; the term means "to make things right."

Find a photo of your father where you can see his eyes. Light a candle. Look into his eyes in the photo and say three times, "I forgive you. Please forgive me. Thank you. I love you." (Adjust as you feel necessary based on your situation.)

The goal is to do this practice for a minimum of 21 days in a row.

Step Six: Break the chain

Be the parental figure you needed to your children. Be attentive, supportive, protective, and present with your children and your family. Be the fatherly figure needed in this world.

Personal insights

My lifelong personal experiences with the mother and father wounds left me in a state of hyper-independence and perfectionism that I continue to struggle with to this day. I've come to accept that I may never reach a point when I'm able to trust and be vulnerable in a relationship. Through the journey, I've been able to love and accept my father for who he is, and I'm grateful for that progress, as it brings great inner peace.

Notes

_____

_____

_____

HEALING THE INNER CHILD

What is the inner child?

The inner child is the childlike part your psyche that influences your thoughts and behaviors as an adult. Ultimately, the parts of your unhealed inner child control your subconscious, which affects how you operate and self-regulate emotionally and physically. The inner child holds painful memories of your past that unconsciously create your present reality. The inner child is typically from the time frame of your childhood prior to reaching puberty. Recognizing and healing the wounded inner child is often the most critical key to spiritual growth and emotional maturity.

Characteristics of a wounded inner child include:

- Addictive personality and behaviors
- Inability to self-regulate
- Reactionary to emotional triggers
- Low self-esteem
- Low self-confidence
- Feeling invisible
- Impulsive behavior

- Anxiety
- Fear of abandonment
- Depression and suppression of emotions
- Inability to accept criticism
- Irrational or immature thinking
- Attachment disorders
- Inability to control emotions
- Negative inner voice
- Difficulty setting boundaries
- Over-identification with pleasing others

How to heal the inner child

Inner child pain generally stems from the parental caregivers, so it's imperative to complete the processes for healing the mother and father wounds first. However, you need to go deeper when addressing the complexities of healing the inner child. Establishing a conscious reclamation of innocence and joy is needed to fuel the spark for lighting up the inner child. As an adult, you will take on the role of re-parenting your inner child to lovingly fulfill your inner child's unmet needs. Providing yourself an environment of safety, comfort, and compassion is foundational for the process. Bringing in the element of playfulness is key for embodying inner peace.

Step One: Reconnect

Reconnect with your inner child by answering these six questions:

1) What was your favorite color as a child?

_____

2) What was your favorite movie as a child? Why?

_____

3) What was your favorite song or band as a child?

_____

4) What was your favorite animal as a child?

_____

5) What was your favorite activity, sport, or hobby?

_____

6) What did you want to be when you grew up?

_____

Step Two: Identify

Identify times as a child when you felt scared, ashamed, or hurt. Listen to your inner child without judgement or shame. Dedicate a few moments every day, for at least a week, to journaling about the feelings of your inner child. See what emotions arise and observe how these moments are tied into how you operate as an adult. Make notes of when these triggers have created repeated thoughts and behavioral patterns throughout your life.

- You may want to write a letter from the voice of your inner child describing what they need.
- You can also write a letter to your inner child from your adult self, giving your inner child the caretaking that they need.

Step Three: "Time travel"

Imagine you are able to time travel as an adult back to the moments you identified in Step Two. Visualize, in detail, yourself as a child. What advice, guidance, or comfort would you give to this younger version of yourself? Perhaps it's just a hug or a safe space to play. Revisit each moment and write about the experiences. This is your chance to give your inner child the parenting they needed.

Step Four: Integrate

To help integrate the healed inner child, adopt healthy daily practices like meditation, journaling, breathwork, stretching, and walking. Also honor your inner child with "play," such as listening to music you love, dancing, games, sports, drawing, painting, and any other hobbies and interests that bring you joy. Integration is not about being productive; it's about embracing the present moment and allowing yourself to feel inner peace.

Personal insights

I avoided working on my inner child for years. I always felt like a mini adult and thought the idea of trying to heal an inner child that I felt never existed was pointless. But I was wrong. I still had a spark of child within me that was craving attention and playfulness. I struggled tremendously with connecting to my inner child. Eventually, I made a list of pastimes that I loved as a child, and at the top of the list was roller-skating. I got goosebumps all over thinking about how much I loved to escape reality by putting on my Walkman and roller-skating around the neighborhood. So, in my mid-forties, I bought a pair of Rollerblades and full body pads and starting Rollerblading around my neighborhood. I allowed myself to let go and embrace the fun of feeling free on my Rollerblades. This experience greatly helped me reconnect to that childlike playfulness my inner child craved.

Notes

_____

_____

_____

HEALING THROUGH THE PROCESS OF GRIEF

What is grief?

Grief is the sorrow of losing someone or something of great importance. Grief can occur after the loss of a loved one, a relationship, a job, a home, health, etc. Many don't realize that grief can run through the subconscious for the loss of relationships and opportunities that did not manifest in our lives. For example, a woman can have deep-seated sadness over never having children. A man can have intense sadness about never finding a spouse. It is important to recognize grief for life situations that we aspired to experience but never achieved. If we don't bring the grief up to the surface, then it will manifest within our subconscious minds, creating undesirable life situations designed to bring our attention to the need for healing.

How to heal through grieving

Everyone processes grief differently, but there are five key stages that are generally universal, per the Kübler-Ross model.[*] These stages are not linear and are experienced in various capacities depending on the individual and the situation. The five

---

[*] Elisabeth Kübler-Ross, *On Death and Dying* (Simon & Schuster/Touchstone, 1969).

stages are denial, anger, bargaining, depression, and acceptance. To heal from a loss, it's important to honor your feelings in each of these stages.

Denial. This is the stage most people dwell in for long periods of time, because we do not want to deal with the pain of loss. Additionally, many of us are stuck in survival mode (fight-or-flight) and cannot focus on healing, so the pain of the loss gets "swept under the rug." It's especially easy to be in denial of sadness for the loss of aspired outcomes not obtained.

Anger. Experiencing a loss can lead to righteous and justified anger. The anger becomes a problem when it is either suppressed or impulsively reactionary. Suppressed anger manifests as depression and makes it difficult to function. Impulsively indulging in expressing anger is destructive. Anger is one of the few emotions fueled with a great deal of energy. Being able to channel the energy of anger in a productive manner is key for releasing it and transmuting it. Transmuting anger in a healthy way can be achieved through exercise, journaling, talk therapy, volunteering, and directing energy into solutions.

Bargaining. Occurring at a point of bleak despair is bargaining, when we will do anything to prevent the loss. This stage can easily lead into a dark night of the soul, where reality seems too painful to bear. Allowing yourself to feel the emotion of desperation is necessary to get to the other side.

Depression. Talk therapy is a key part of working through depression over a loss. I can't imagine being able to heal from depression without the release of talk therapy and guidance from a trusted practitioner. Allowing yourself to purge the sadness through crying and feeling your raw emotions is necessary to move on from depression. All the sorrowful emotions from the loss must come to the surface.

Acceptance. The final stage is accepting the loss, when the healing can begin to integrate and process throughout your mind, body, and spirit. Acceptance brings fresh perspectives and innerstandings about the loss that you couldn't see during the other stages. Once acceptance is reached, you enter into a space of new beginnings.

Personal insights

I've grieved the loss of a marriage, jobs, homes, pets, and friendships. Throughout my healing journey, I learned that some of the most important grieving I needed to do was grieving the loss of the experiences I didn't have. For example, grieving the loss of my childhood and never being able to feel joy. Grieving the loss of never experiencing a truly intimate romantic relationship. Grieving the loss of not having parents I could trust or share my life with. Grieving that I spent most of my life in survival mode trying to make ends meet.

Bringing these losses to the surface really gave me clarity about how to direct my focus towards what I wanted to create in life.

I found acceptance to be incredibly difficult, because I thought accepting the loss meant giving up on all future possibilities. But that is not the case. Acceptance put me in the present moment, providing freedom from the pains of sorrow that were dwelling deep within my subconscious. Bringing those painful losses into my conscious mind is when I felt the powerful impact of healing.

A friend of mine who specializes in homeopathy recommended using ignatia to assist with the grieving processing (200c, two times per day). I found ignatia to help with healing grief.

Notes

_____

_____

_____

HEALING FOR THE EMPATH

What is an empath?

An empath is someone who absorbs the feelings and emotions of others. Being empathic means merging with another's emotions in a compassionate manner. Having empathy is being able to sense the feelings of others. Often, people with great empathy feel responsible for others' feelings and experiences.

How does one become an empath

The traits of empathy commonly develop early in childhood as a means of survival during a chaotic upbringing. In order to prevent conflict, children become adept at identifying patterns and energetic signatures in their surroundings. Empaths often operate in a state of hypervigilance, or heightened alertness, which is an effect of trauma. They become gifted in interpreting verbal and nonverbal communication and develop strong intuition.

Empaths & narcissists

Highly empathic people often attract narcissists in relationships. Narcissists, consciously or subconsciously, target empaths. Why does this happen? It happens because of the law of polarity, which states: "Everything is Dual; everything has poles;

everything has its pair of opposites; like and unlike are the same; opposites are identical in nature, but different in degree; extremes meet; all truths are but half-truths; all paradoxes may be reconciled."[†] Essentially, what the law of polarity states is that everything in our reality is dual, everything exists as a pair of opposites on the same continuum or spectrum, and the difference is in the variations of the degree and vibration.

Narcissists and empaths have personality traits on the opposite ends of the same spectrum. Narcissists have the same core childhood wounding, but they manifest and cope with their pain in different ways. Empaths are overly sensitive to others' feelings; narcissists cope by elevating themselves without consideration for others' feelings. Their personalities become defined on the opposite ends of the spectrum, but, believe it or not, they both have elements of the other within them. Empaths identify with being able to read and absorb other people's feelings and energy, and they often feel they have to be the ones to fix everything. But guess what? That identification is somewhat egoic, putting themselves in superior situations and on the narcissists' sides. They have to be able to read energy and other people's emotions well in order to act on their need to control and surpass.

The positive side to empathy

Having empathy for others is part of embracing the human experience. As humans, we have a wide range of emotions, and being able to connect with each other on an emotional level creates the space for bonding, trust, love, and spiritual growth. Empathy leads to having strong intuition and psychic abilities. Empathy allows for deeper innerstanding of another person's experience. Having empathic abilities can also improve one's ability to expand their perspective and viewpoint.

---

† Three Initiates, *The Kybalion: A Study of The Hermetic Philosophy of Ancient Egypt and Greece* (Yogi Publication Society, 1908), Part II, Section 4.

The negative side to empathy

Absorbing the energy of others can create severe exhaustion, depression, and anxiety. Many empaths feel energetically drained after social encounters. Hypervigilance and disassociation can plague an empath and create chronic fatigue syndrome. Empaths have often been known to spend their time and energy trying to fix problems for others while neglecting themselves. A dark side of empathy is one that empaths don't want to identify with, and that is egoic identification. When people identify as empaths, they limit the essences of their true selves. Additionally, this identification can often subtly position empaths as superior to others because they have empathic abilities.

Another dark side of having strong empathy is a lack of independence, because empaths' feelings are dependent on others around them. When others are sad, they are sad; when others are happy, they are happy. Those with strong empathy may lack the ability to control or perceive their own feelings and may experience projective identification, where they adopt the emotions of others.

How to heal & integrate "being an empath"

Start with awareness

The first step to a healthy integration of your empathic traits is to identify key moments in your life when the energy of others controlled you. You may realize the energy of others has dominated the majority of your life decisions.

Helpful prompts

- List situations in your life when you compromised yourself in order to please others.

_____

_____

_____

o How did these situations make you feel after the fact?

_____

_____

_____

o If you could go back in time to those situations knowing what you know now, what would you tell the previous version of yourself?

_____

_____

_____

- Can you remember a time you dealt with confrontation head on?

_____

_____

_____

o What was the result?

_____

_____

_____

o How did that make you feel?

_____

_____

_____

• Have you ever been able to provide sympathy and comfort for another without feeling drained?

_____

_____

_____

• Can you list times in your life when you made important decisions based solely on what was right for you, setting aside the influence of others?

_____

_____

_____

Clear the empath label

Over-identifying with being an empath creates a false self that is essentially egoic in nature. Cease identifying yourself as an empath and start seeing yourself as whole and healed. Also, cease using your identity as an empath as an excuse for not healing or for having problems in your life. The way in which you respond to others is your responsibility, not theirs.

This step may take some time to settle in, as letting go of the empath identity may be painful. You will still embrace empathy, but you will not let it control you.

Helpful prompts

- List the times you've used being an empath as an excuse.

_____

_____

_____

- Have you felt triggered by any part of this empathic healing?

_____

_____

_____

o Write down the triggers and why you feel triggered.

_____

_____

_____

Visualize healthy empathic embodiment

The second step is to visualize the version of yourself that embodies healthy empathy. This image of your whole, healthy, energetic self will help create the metaphysical bridge from where you are now to where you want to be. This means visualizing yourself caring for others and helping them with solutions rather than taking on their energy. **It's vital to innerstand that absorbing**

another's pain does not alleviate the pain for them; it just spreads the pain out over more people.

Helpful prompts

- Identify specific people who always make you feel drained after spending time together.

_____

_____

_____

    o List how you can start setting healthy boundaries.

_____

_____

_____

    o Identify ways you can help others with solutions but not take on their problems as your own.

_____

_____

_____

    o Visualize yourself feeling energized after meeting with them because you just provided assistance to them without sacrificing yourself, creating a win-win outcome.

_____

_____

_____

- Imagine the kind of social life you would live if you didn't get drained by others' energy. What does that version of yourself look like and feel like?

_____

_____

_____

Work on the core wounding: FEAR

As mentioned previously, the core wounding of empaths generally stems from instability and trauma in childhood. The core wound is based in fear—fear of survival, fear of rejection, fear of abandonment, fear of painful consequences for "rocking the boat."

Therefore, the antidote to the core wounding is finding safety, security, and confidence in being your true self. Feeling safe is paramount for healing out-of-balance empathy.

The higher self-activation is a critical piece of feeling safe. Once you are comfortable with who you are and your true self, you can fall back into a space of security in any situation.

This means that you will face rejection, abandonment, and backlash from others who may not like your new healthy boundaries. However, you will never truly feel free until you feel safe to be yourself. In part, this step is about self–re-discovery and self-respect.

Personal insights

Years ago, when I first learned about empaths, I was overcome with relief that I was not alone in having these traits that made me feel socially awkward. I felt validated and grateful to finally have an innerstanding of why I felt so different from other people and why I felt drained after social events. It helped me innerstand why I felt safer being alone.

The journey of setting healthy boundaries was tumultuous for me because it involved setting boundaries with my family, who did not take well to these new limits I placed on our relationships. I suffered through what I feared most—rejection, abandonment, and "rocking the boat." But, as a result, I gained incredible personal freedom and self-remembrance of my spirit. I became stronger, calmer, and happier. Ironically, setting boundaries to protect my energy made me even more capable of helping, caring, and empathizing with others in a healthy manner.

While I was going through my own empathic healing and integration, the metaphor that helped me the most was the image of sending a drowning person a life raft vs. swimming out and drowning with them. It helped me innerstand that absorbing another's pain doesn't heal their pain. It may make them feel better temporarily, but it does not fix their core wounding. Additionally, the innerstanding that I can't help others if I'm drowning too motivated me to set boundaries and protect my energy field without feeling guilty.

Notes

_____

_____

_____

THE DARK NIGHT OF THE SOUL & SHADOW WORK

The dark night of the soul and shadow work go hand-in-hand because they are intertwined. Shadow work often triggers a dark night of the soul. Doing shadow work doesn't necessarily mean that you will go into a dark night of the soul, but navigating through the dark night of the soul always requires shadow work. This intensive introspection and self-reflection sets up the opportunity to take profound responsibility for your low frequency thoughts and behaviors. The dark night of the soul is a painful phase you experience when uncovering truths about yourself and the world that were previously masked. This process requires realizing that your ego, or false self, has shaped most of your life decisions and behavior. Throughout the dark night of the soul, you may grapple with how you've been controlled by false projections, social conditioning, and 3-D matrix programming. Realizations that you haven't been living an authentic life can cause a break down, with feelings of hopelessness, failure, and despair. The dark night of the soul typically occurs after a major life catalyst event, such as the death of a loved one, loss of a job, divorce, trauma healing, etc.

The purpose of the dark night of the soul is transformation. It creates profound introspection and self-awareness on a spiritual level. After a dark night of the soul, you may never see the world the same again. For some, the dark night of the soul can last years as they resist the pains of transformation and letting go of what no longer serves them. For others, the dark night of the soul is short but still equally impactful. It's not uncommon to experience more than one dark night of the soul throughout a lifetime. Each dark night of the soul serves as an opportunity to catapult your spiritual maturity to a higher level.

I consider the process of the dark night of the soul a rebirth and metamorphosis, similar to a caterpillar going into a dark, secluded chrysalis and emerging as a butterfly.

Navigating the dark night of the soul

During a dark night of the soul, it's easy to feel lost, alone, and depressed. Below, I share some tools to help guide you through the storm and bring you safely to the other side of the transformation. Because the dark night of the soul is unique to each individual, the tools are not in order of steps; use your intuition about which order to execute these in based on what you are experiencing.

Write. Journaling your emotions is key. Use your own handwriting instead of typing. Don't hold back on writing down your feelings—you can always rip up and throw away your writings if you are scared to hold onto them. Writing down the feelings of darkness that surface is necessary for purging and letting go. Don't judge yourself. Let your true feelings flow onto the paper without a filter.

Feel. Let yourself feel without fear. Feel sad, feel angry, feel guilty, feel frustrated. Know that you're safe and you are not acting on these feelings; you are giving them recognition so they can be transformed.

Purge. Let yourself cry. Let yourself sweat. A sweat lodge is a fantastic option for accelerating the process of the dark night of the soul, as it purges trapped energies. Fasting during this time can help accelerate the process as well. Fasting purges toxins physically and energetically.

Observe. Take yourself out of the moment and view your life situation from a 30,000-ft. viewpoint. Changing your perspective can open the door for the transformation to occur. You may see new solutions and parts of yourself that you never appreciated before. You may see certain situations from the perspectives of those whom you may have once thought of as enemies. Try to remain emotionally detached while observing in order to keep your emotions from blocking out the full 360-degree view.

Identify. Can you identify the shadow aspects that are surfacing? Here are some common shadow aspects that subconsciously run the show in our lives:

- Jealousy
- Shame
- Sadness
- Anger
- Cold-heartedness
- Judgement of others
- Vanity
- Pride
- Lust
- False entitlement
- Perfectionism
- Savior Complexes
- Victimhood
- Martyrdom
- Fear

Purge the parasitic energies that no longer serve you

Once you've worked on the steps above, you will want to officially release these shadow aspects. This takes place in the form of recognizing the shadow aspect, taking responsibility for it, and then replacing it with another quality that is in alignment with your true self.

Three-step purging process:

Repent. During this purge, you will repent each shadow aspect three times. Since the word *repent* means to turn around 180 degrees, don't feel that this is a shameful or a guilt-ridden process.

Renounce. Then, you will renounce each shadow aspect three times. The word *renounce* means committing to not doing a behavior any longer.

Announce. Lastly, you will need to fill the void of each attribute immediately, so you will announce a replacement three times.

A very detailed outline of this process, plus a video walkthrough link, is included in the Appendix.

Personal insights

In *Remember Your Torch*, I share my personal experiences with the dark night of the soul in great detail. One of the techniques that helped me get in touch with my suppressed suffering and pain was journaling my emotions in the third person. For example, "I feel sad for the Katie that never felt loved and always felt afraid." This journaling technique really helps when you have become disassociated from the painful trauma of your own experiences.

Remember, battling through a dark night of the soul is the journey of a truly courageous spiritual warrior and not for the faint of heart. Give yourself recognition and appreciation for battling your inner demons head on and take comfort in knowing that this is part of the human experience. You are not alone.

Notes

_____

_____

_____

HIGHER SELF/TRUE SELF ACTIVATION

Higher self vs. true self

It's important to balance shadow work with activations for the higher self and the true self. The higher self and true self are essentially the same; however, I define the higher self as the eternal part of you that acts as a guide for your experiences on Earth. There are levels to the higher self, as you have multiple versions of yourself throughout the different densities that make up the universal construct.

I define the true self similarly to the higher self, but this is the eternal part of your soul that is within your current 3-D physical self. It is your connection, or link, to the higher self. I refer the higher self as the part of you that is outside the time and space construct and the true self as the part of you that is inside the construct. By activating your true self on the 3-D Earth plane, you are connecting to the consciousness of your higher self, which has a larger view of the playing field, so to speak. Your true self is the pure essence of your divine nature as a spark and fractal of the Aviaya, or God, Source, or Creator. Finding your true frequency will unlock your communication channel to your higher self.

The inner child & sparking the true self

Once again, the need for inner child work arises, as there is a strong connection between the true self and the inner child. In order to spark and activate the true self, you need to remember the people, places, and experiences that made you feel alive. Reflect on the times when you were so happy and immersed in an activity that you lost track of time. This process is a true reignition of the flame that fuels your life. Over time, with the 3-D false matrix programming, the flames of our souls may dim. Use this opportunity to breathe life back into your divine spark.

Take comfort that your higher self already has everything mapped out—you just need to follow your heart and create the bridge.

Process

Take your time to answer the 10 questions below. This may take several days for you to complete, depending on your situation. The questions are designed to trigger and activate the spark within your soul. They will help shift your perspective so that you can see a new path and feel enlivened on a new level. This process is designed to take you from existing to living.

Questions:

1) If you knew today was your last day on Earth, what memories would you hold most precious? What would you wish you had spent more time on? What would you have loved the most?

_____

_____

_____

2) Can you remember times when you were so happy that you couldn't wait to get out of bed in the morning? Write about those experiences below.

_____

_____

_____

3) If money were not an issue, how would you want to spend your time?

_____

_____

_____

4) What is your favorite hobby, sport, talent, or pastime?

_____

_____

_____

5) If you could go back in time and visit your younger self, what advice would you give them at age 8? Age 15? Age 20?

_____

_____

_____

6) List at least five attributes, characteristics, talents, and/or innate gifts that are unique to you.

_____

_____

_____

7) Who is the most influential person in your life, and why?

_____

_____

_____

8) When was the last time you laughed uncontrollably, and what was the situation?

_____

_____

_____

9) What kind of person do you want to be?

_____

_____

_____

10) What's holding you back from being the person you want to be?

_____

_____

_____

Personal insights

The most impactful questions for my personal journey were questions 9 and 10. As I navigated my healing journey, I battled feeling suppressed by the false 3-D matrix system. I felt suffocated and forced to live a life chained to my job in order to survive. I had a major breakthrough when going through this process myself, and I realized that the dark control structures of the 3-D false matrix could not control my ability to be the person I wanted to be. This is because the person I wanted to be was kind, compassionate, and in service to others. No matter what job I held or what situation I faced, I was in control of my choice to operate from that place. My perspective shifted when I had the epiphany that the only person holding me back from being the person I wanted to be was me.

Notes

_____

_____

_____

HEALING FOR TARGETED INDIVIDUALS

What is a targeted individual?

A targeted individual (TI) is an individual who is heavily tracked, surveilled, and stalked by the Deep State or private agencies. Targeted Individual programs instill intimidation, fear, and paranoia within their targets. These programs use synthetic telepathy and thought monitoring to manipulate their targets. The Deep State, Shadow Governments, and three-letter agencies possess technology to both read thoughts and transmit them into the minds of targeted individuals. They can even have messages subliminally embedded in television programming and tailor the feed to mirror or interact with the targeted individuals' thought processes.

How to heal from being a targeted individual

The whistle-blowers of targeted individual programs, such as Robert Duncan, PhD., state that liberating yourself from such programs requires you to elevate your consciousness and frequency. I attribute this type of elevation in consciousness to a reality shift. The universal laws of correspondence and vibration come into effect when shifting your reality and making the changes internally to manifest the external outcomes you desire. You can't control whether or not you are being targeted, but you can change how you react, which is your key to liberation.

How to shift your reality

Shifting your reality needs to occur on all subtle bodies of your existences: mental, physical, emotional, and spiritual. These subtle bodies need to be in alignment in order for you to shift your frequency out of the TI programming. Below is a guide to help you shift into a higher consciousness. Be sure to be patient with yourself through this journey, as it can take time.

Mental body shift:

Accept. You are in an unfair situation being a TI. You won't be able to shift your reality until you accept your circumstances and work from where you are in the present moment.

Redirect. Thoughts create your reality. Recognize looping thought patterns that evoke feelings of paranoia, fear, and anger. Every time they arise, focus on redirecting your thoughts. Have an image ready to pull up, such as a beloved pet or happy memory, to start conditioning your brain to automatically redirect itself to a high vibrational thought pattern when negative thoughts creep in.

Physical body shift:

Control. Focus on what you can control regarding your physical body. Prioritize healthy foods, exercise, and sleep. Make baby steps towards your health goals so that they become a part of your everyday routine; don't try to make big adjustments too quickly. Talk walks in nature, get a massage, do somatic yoga—all of which are designed to help relax your central nervous system so it can heal and live at a higher vibration.

Detox. Do parasite cleanses, heavy metal detoxes, and fasts. Keeping your body as clean as possible is critical. Detoxing also includes detoxing from social media and toxic programming. Try to limit your engagement with the media, social sites, and TV; all of these are designed to keep you in a lower frequency.

Emotional body shift:

> **Feel.** The remote frequencies are going to play off your trapped emotions. Allow yourself to release feelings of sadness, anger, resentment, frustration, victimization, etc. Going through the shadow work process outlined earlier in this workbook will help you release trapped emotions.

> **Laugh.** Make a conscious effort to laugh every day. Find a show or comedian that always makes you laugh and tune in for five minutes or less at least once a day. Try to see the humor in life around you when you can.

Spiritual body shift:

> **Connect.** Make time every day, even as short as two minutes, to connect with your true self in order to tune into your resonant frequency. Instead of spending time focused on your problem, work with the Aviaya by asking for solutions and opportunities for change.

> **Acknowledge.** No matter how dark your situation becomes, make it a daily practice to list three things that make you feel grateful. These can be as simple as having a roof above your head, having running water, or having the ability to walk. Don't take anything for granted.

Support

Talk therapy and support groups provide invaluable assistance in the process of reality shifting. Choose a practitioner that you can fully trust. I recommend finding practitioners through the United Intentions Foundation. Targeted Justice is another organization that provides information on support groups and assistance with life as a TI. Links to both websites can be found in the Resources section of this workbook.

Personal insights

The targeted programming doesn't necessarily ever go away once you've been a TI, but how you handle it changes the game completely. In my experience, once I stopped thinking of myself as a victim, I accepted my situation and faced it directly.

Instead of focusing on the things I couldn't control, I put my focus and energy on the things I could control: all the items listed above. Taking my attention off the problem and focusing on the solution made me unaffected by the TI programming.

Keeping a gratitude journal was essential for me to shift my reality. Even during my darkest moments, I always made time every day to journal three things that made me feel grateful. Being able to harness the power of gratitude in times of desperation fuels transformation and transmutes negative energy into creating a positive outcome.

Notes

_____

_____

_____

CO-CREATION WITH THE AVIAYA

I use the term Aviaya (pronounced av-EYE-ah) to convey the concept of an omnipotent universal source that breathes life into all of creation. The Aviaya is our connection to the one true divine essence of creation beyond the veils of the illusion. Aviaya is the breath of spirit that embodies the soul, which, in turn, animates the body. This is the energy that ignites your internal flame. Learning how to communicate with the life force energy of creation will open up new doors for manifesting your life in harmony with your spirit.

Below are some examples of how you can begin co-creating with the Aviaya:

Ask. Make an intention, out loud or silently, asking for assistance and guidance in connecting with the Aviaya, or whatever word you choose to use for the life force energy.

Share. Set aside five minutes a day to get into a still, sacred mind space and share your thoughts with the Aviaya as if you are talking to a friend. Tell them about your day, the highs and lows, the things you love about this world, and the things you don't care for about this world. You may be surprised at what surfaces in your reflective thoughts.

Light a small candle while doing this practice to deepen your connection through the portal of the flame.

Play. Have time every day to do something that honors your inner child and brings you joy. Acknowledge the presence of the Aviaya when you are happy, as this will generate more joyful experiences.

Receive. Be receptive to seeing signs that you are in sync with creation. These will manifest as natural synchronicities. Give gratitude for all of these signs and synchronicities, as they will help guide you to living life in alignment with your soul's desires.

Personal insights

There are three times during the day in which I love to connect to the Aviaya. First, I like to sit outside on my porch with a candle early in the morning, around five a.m., and connect to the Aviaya in silence through the flame. Second, I like to take a walk at midday without my phone or distractions, and I visualize myself walking with the Aviaya energy as I share my thoughts and open up to receive. Third, I love to sit outside at nighttime and gaze up at the stars while I share my day with the Aviaya. I share what I love about this creation on Earth, as well as the things I find to be nuisances. These sacred moments throughout the day have assisted me with my own intuition and walking my life's path in alignment with loving service to all of creation.

Notes

_____

_____

_____

RESOURCES

Somatic Yoga:

Brett Larkin Yoga, YouTube Channel: www.youtube.com/@BrettLarkinYoga

Homeopathy

Lisa Rooney, Integrative Homeopathic Certification: www.vibrantlife247.com

Breath Work

Breathe with Sandy, YouTube Channel: www.youtube.com/@BreatheWithSandy

Universal Laws

Three Initiates. *The Kybalion*. Yogi Publication Society, 1908.

Grief

Kübler-Ross, Elisabeth. *On Death and Dying*. Simon & Schuster/Touchstone, 1969.

Targeted Individual Resources

United Intentions Foundation Freeing Hearts and Minds Relief Fund:
https://www.unitedintentions.org/survivors

Targeted Justice: https://targetedjustice.com/

Reconciliation & Forgiveness

Rafaelovich, Kamailelauli'l, LMT, R, MBA, Ihaleakala Hew Len, PhD., and Momilani
Ramstrum, PhD. *BLUE ICE: The Relationship with The Self: Self I-Dentity through Ho'oponopono, MsKr SITH Conversations, Book 1*. Bingboard Consulting, LLC, 2014.

APPENDIX

Parasitic Energy Attachment Removal

The Earth Bishop YouTube channel features the walkthrough video, entitled "Parasitic Entity Attachment Removal and Embodiment of the True Self." www.youtube.com/@EarthBishop

Here is the process in great detail:

1) Prepare yourself & do shadow work

   - Prepare yourself by doing shadow work and identifying the areas within yourself where you are feeding vampiric or negative energies. Have a replacement plan for addictive or destructive looping behaviors and thought patterns.
   - These will be the areas that you will use in the "Repent" and "Renounce & announce" sections below.

2) Create your space for conducting the protocol

   - Make your area comfortable, clean, and clear to prevent any distractions, interruptions, or peripheral interference.

3) Call in protection

   - Call in protection from your higher self and your guides, guardians, or ascended teachers/masters. You can also say "I put on the full armor of God." I recommend calling in Mother Mary.

4) Clear your energetic space from interference

   - Do a clearing of your surrounding sacred sovereign space.

5) Breathe, relax & ground into your body

- Do a breathing exercise. For example: Inhale through your nose for four counts, hold for four counts, exhale through your mouth for eight counts, and hold out for an additional four counts. Repeat three times. (Holding a longer exhale will automatically relax your parasympathetic nervous system.)

6) Announce permissions in the astral

- "I now enter this clearing in full trust as a child of the one true Source/God/Creator. With the power of Yeshua/Eesa/Jesus and his embodiment of the Christ Consciousness, I thank Yeshua/Eesa/Jesus and ask him to act on my behalf in the astral and spirit realms."
- If you do not feel comfortable calling on Yeshua, use another fifth density or higher ascended being.

7) Repent

- "I am sorry, and I repent for _____."
- Example: "I am sorry, and I repent for all the times I withheld forgiveness."
- Repeat three times for each area identified in step one.

8) Renounce & announce

- "I renounce _____, and I announce _____."
- Example: "I renounce withholding forgiveness, and I announce granting forgiveness and compassion for those who have hurt me."
- Repeat three times for each area.

9) Affirm abolishment of entity-attachments

"I have fully repented and renounced all transgressions before Source/God/ Creator, and I now abolish the rights of all demonic forces and entities connected to my sacred energy to stay attached to me."

"Yeshua/Eesa/Jesus, I, (say your full legal name), ask for your assistance, and I give you the permission and power to act on my behalf to drive out and cut all cords and attachments to parasitic and demonic entities and either take them to their next stages of evolution or return them to Source/God/Creator for transmutation."

"I shine the Christed light of truth on all demonic forces and entities, organic and inorganic, that have taken residency in my mind-body-spirit complex, and, in the name of Yeshua/Eesa/Jesus, I now bind up these energies and their sources so they cannot harm me any further. All the cords to any outside spirits are completely severed and cast off in the name of Jesus Christ."

"In the name of Yeshua/Eesa/Jesus, I dry up all the waters from which any demonic forces have been drinking. With the power of Christ's light, I diminish the kingdoms that any and all demonic forces have built, and I eradicate all cords, portals, and parasitic attachments that were connected to my mind-body-spirit complex throughout the morphogenetic field across all timelines and dimensions."

"In the name of Yeshua/Eesa/Jesus, I abolish all agreements and contracts that infringe on my sovereignty and my sacred space."

To break generational contracts and curses, repeat the below line three times:

"In the name of Yeshua/Eesa/Jesus, I break and free myself from all generational contracts and curses."

10) Final command cast out

"With the power of Yeshua/Eesa/Jesus and the Christed light, I cast out all negative entities, organic and inorganic, from my mind, body, and spirit. I command all demonic forces to leave my mind, body, and spirit immediately."

Repeat this three times.

11) Receive

"As a child of the divine Aviaya/Source/God/Creator (or whatever word(s) you choose), I receive with every fiber of my being infinite and unconditional love, compassion, and grace from the nurturing divine mother of creation, and protection and infinite love from the divine father. I wholly accept their love, and I strengthen our connection. I install, anchor, lock, and seal the frequency of infinite unconditional love to deeply heal all wounded aspects of myself. May I feel and know my own worthiness as a divine being of creation."

12) Seal

"I pronounce the completion of all energic transformations made today, and I anchor, lock, and seal my purification and my sovereignty throughout the morphogenetic field, across all planes and times of existence. And so it is."

13) Give thanks

Give thanks and gratitude for the assistance of all guides, guardians, angels, and Yeshua/Eesa/Jesus.

14) Aftercare for integration

- Drink plenty of water
- Get lots of rest

- Eat clean, healthy foods and avoid sugar
- Stay grounded
- Move your body and keep the energy flowing: exercise, walking, stretching, yoga, massage
- Be gentle with yourself; spontaneous crying, exhaustion, and feeling emotional are normal symptoms
- Develop a daily habit of protecting and clearing your energy field, as well as grounding, self-reflecting, and receiving